AF228433

JAMES–JUDE

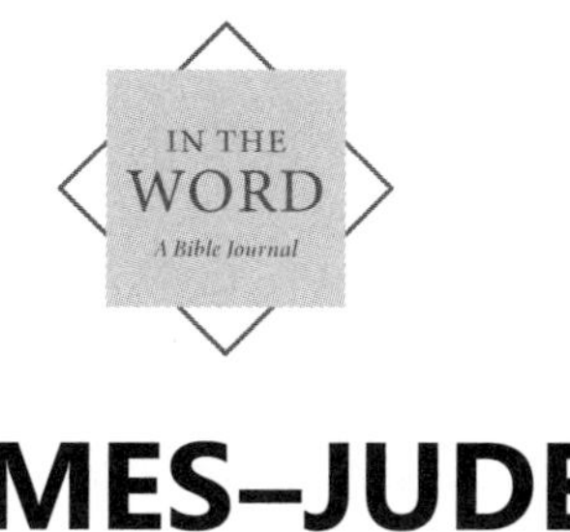

JAMES–JUDE

Rob Wynalda, Joel R. Beeke,
and Paul M. Smalley

REFORMATION HERITAGE BOOKS
Grand Rapids, Michigan

Reformation Heritage Books
3070 29th St. SE
Grand Rapids, MI 49512
616-977-0889
orders@heritagebooks.org
www.heritagebooks.org

25 26 27 28 29 30/11 10 9 8 7 6 5 4 3 2

ISBN 979-8-88686-172-3

PREFACE

In Deuteronomy 17, Moses leaves final instructions concerning the future of Israel. As a prophet of God, he foretells that Israel will set a king over the nation (v. 14). This king must be an Israelite, not a foreigner (v. 15), and is forbidden to do certain things (vv. 16–17). In verse 18, Moses transitions to what the king should do. The king is commanded not to simply acquire a copy of the law (the entire book of Deuteronomy), but to handwrite his own copy of the law. The purpose was so that he would read it, fear the Lord, obey, avoid pride, not deviate, and enjoy a long reign (vv. 19–20; cf. Prov. 4:20–27).

More than three thousand years later, modern educators have discovered that students who write out notes by hand have a much higher retention rate than those who simply hear or visually read the information. Apparently, God knew this to be true for the kings of Israel also.

This series of books, known as The Bible Journal, was born from the insight found in Deuteronomy 17:18. Your Bible Journal gives you the opportunity to write out your own copy of a portion of the Holy Scriptures, just as the ancient kings of Israel were instructed to do. Writing out the words of the Bible helps a person to engage the Word of God by slowing down the process of reading the text. Writing answers to the discussion questions also helps you to thoughtfully engage the text. Furthermore, by completing a journal, you leave a legacy to pass on to future generations your insights and personal applications of the text (Deut. 6:6–9; Ps. 78:4–7).

To prepare you to meditate on this portion of the Holy Scriptures, we include an introduction to the book of the Bible to help you understand more thoroughly the Bible book you are about to write out in full. Study Questions and Devotional Reflections have been added after the blank pages set aside for copying each chapter of God's Word. The Study Questions focus on individual verses to keep you thinking about what you are writing, and the Devotional Reflections are designed to help you focus on a few of the major takeaways for your practical Christian life that each Bible chapter provides. We wish to thank Reformation Heritage Books for allowing us to use material drawn from *The Reformation Heritage KJV Study Bible* for the Bible Introduction material and for the Devotional Reflections. The Study Questions have been written by the authors of *The Bible Journal*. Thus, The Bible Journal walks you through a process of getting acquainted with a book of the Bible, copying a chapter by hand, reflecting on the meaning and application of that chapter, and then repeating the process for the next chapter. Families, friends, and small groups can work through a journal together, discussing their meditations for mutual edification as guided by the discussion questions.

The mass production of the Bible since the invention of the printing press has greatly blessed the world. However, there is also great benefit for Bible readers of all ages in following the Deuteronomy 17:18 principle and producing your own handwritten copy of the text.

May God richly bless you in writing and learning His Word through The Bible Journal (Rom. 1:16).

—Rob Wynalda, Joel R. Beeke, and Paul M. Smalley

Introduction to the Book of
JAMES

AUTHORSHIP: The author of the book of James simply identifies himself as, "James, a servant of God and of the Lord Jesus Christ" (1:1). While there are upwards of six different people named James in the New Testament, we can be rather sure that James the half brother of Jesus is the author of this book (Mark 6:3; Gal. 1:19). First, James was one of the pillars of the church, and held a prominent role in Jerusalem; lacking further specification, early readers would have assumed "James" would have been *this* James. Second, scholars have examined the sentence structure and words spoken by James in Acts 15:13–21 and that of the epistle and have found striking similarity. Third, due to the contents of this book, it is clear that James was written at an early date but also by a date when persecution, suffering, and oppression were widespread in the early church. This fits what we know about James, the brother of Christ. Finally, church history has well documented that James the half brother of Jesus authored this book at an early date.

What do we know about James? During Christ's ministry on earth, James and Christ's other half brothers did not believe in Christ (John 7:5). After His resurrection, Christ made a special appearance to James (1 Cor. 15:7), which may have marked the turning point for him. Afterward, we find him in prayer with the believing followers of Christ (Acts 1:14). It is worth noting that nowhere in this letter does James highlight his physical relationship to Christ. Instead, he is content to refer to himself as "a servant of God and of the Lord Jesus Christ" (James 1:1).

DATE: There are many who consider James to be a very early Christian document, perhaps the first book written in the New Testament canon. As already pointed out, by the time James wrote his epistle, Christianity had been established long enough for there to be not only persecution and suffering but also oppression of some in the church by others in the church. At the same time, James does not refer to the Jerusalem Council (AD 48 or 49). The influx of Gentiles into the church caused some major tension in the early church. However, this tension is absent from the epistle of James. Thus, it was probably written somewhere in the early to mid-40s.

THEME: The difference between pure and vain religion.

PURPOSE: To expose the myth that the Christian life is not costly, while encouraging true believers to live in close fellowship with the Lord.

SYNOPSIS
The Contribution of James to Redemptive Revelation
James shows how times of testing are good at showing whether our religion is true or false.

1. True religion comes down from God and is established in the heart by spiritual regeneration (1:17). Carnal religion springs from the heart, which brings forth sin, and sin brings forth death (v. 15).

2. True religion arises from "the engrafted word," which saves the soul (v. 21). Carnal religion proceeds from "the wrath of man" (v. 20).

3. True religion, when tested, is patient, constant, and God-glorifying (vv. 2–18). Vain religion wavers, is unstable in everything, and fades away (vv. 2–18).

4. True religion is faith working by love (2:14–26). It keeps itself unspotted from the world (1:27), respects not persons (2:1–3), bridles the tongue (3:5–12), humbles itself before God (4:8–10), relies on God (vv. 13–17), and is fervent in prayer (5:13–20). On the other hand, vain religion does not work (2:4–26), promotes envying (3:13–18), lusts (4:1–12), and is indulgent (5:5).

5. True religion has its perfect work (1:4) and leads to peace (3:18) and precious fruits unto the coming again of the Lord (5:7). Carnal religion will be judged without mercy (2:13), and will fall into condemnation (5:12).

6. True religion saves from death (5:20) and will lift the humble believer up (4:10). Carnal religion will lead to death (5:20) along with the devil and his hosts (4:7).

OUTLINE

I. Address of the Epistle (1:1)

II. The Tests of True Religion (1:2–27)
    A. The Benefits of a Tried Faith (1:2–8)
    B. Two Tests: Poverty and Temptation (1:9–15)
    C. True Religion Distinguished from False (1:16–27)

III. The Demonstration of True Religion (2:1–26)
    A. A Case against Favoritism (2:1–13)
    B. A Case for True Faith (2:14–26)

IV. The Subtlety of Sin (3:1–18)
    A. Sin in Speaking (3:1–12)
    B. The Sin of Striving (3:13–18)

V. A Call to Humility (4:1–17)
    A. The Problem: Pride (4:1–3)
    B. Humility before God (4:4–10)
    C. Humility Regarding Others (4:11–12)
    D. Humility Regarding the Future (4:13–17)

VI. Life in Light of the End (5:1–20)
    A. A Warning to the Rich (5:1–6)
    B. An Encouragement to Patience (5:7–11)
    C. The Value of Prayer (5:12–20)

Notes

1

2

3

4

5

6

7

8

Notes

9

10

11

12

13

14

15

16

Notes

17

18

19

20

21

22

23

24

Notes

25

26

27

STUDY QUESTIONS

1. Verses 2–4: How should believers regard their trials? Why?

2. Verse 5: What promise does God give to encourage us to pray?

3. Verse 8: What warning is given here (James 4:4, 8)?

4. Verse 12: Why does James say that the person who perseveres through trials is blessed?

5. Verse 13: Why should we never say that God tempts us to sin?

6. Verse 17: What does this teach us about God's nature and work?

7. Verses 19–21: With what attitude should we receive God's Word?

8. Verses 23–24: To what may we compare a person who hears the Word but does not do it?

9. Verses 26–27: What are crucial differences between worthless religion and pure religion?

DEVOTIONAL REFLECTIONS

1. Trials for Christians are not a matter of if, but "when"(v. 2). Despite what some teach and many imagine, Christians are not promised an exemption from trials. We can, however, face these trials with joy because we know that God has designed them for our good (Rom. 8:28, 32) and as a means of refining us. Christ endured His greatest trial, the cross, because of the joy that was set before him (Heb. 12:2–3). What trials are you facing? How can you count them as joy?

2. We must learn to hate deception and love the truth (vv. 16, 18, 21–22). In a day and age when skepticism is considered virtuous and agnosticism humble, we need to remember that God has revealed His truth in His Word. By the truth lost sinners are born again, by the truth they are saved, and by the truth they live in true happiness and freedom. Therefore, let us receive the truth with meekness.

3. James warns against worldly Christianity (v. 26). Carnal religion has no problem immersing itself in the world, which contaminates with its impurities. On the other hand, the believer seeks, by the grace of God, "to keep himself unspotted from the world" (v. 27). The Christian's affections should be with those who are in need, such as widows and orphans, rather than with the sinful pleasures the world offers, which only defile.

Notes

1

2

3

4

5

6

7

Notes

8

9

10

11

12

13

14

15

Notes

16

17

18

19

20

21

22

Notes

23

24

25

26

STUDY QUESTIONS

1. Verses 1–3: What kind of partiality (or favoritism) is James rebuking here?

2. Verse 5: Why is it foolish to despise the poor?

3. Verse 8: What does the law of God require us to do to our neighbor? What does that have to do with the subject of this passage of Scripture?

4. Verses 12–13: How should the doctrine of judgment day affect our speech and behavior?

5. Verse 17: What is true of faith in God if it produces no works of mercy to others?

6. Verse 19: Who also believes in God, but it does them no good?

7. Verse 21: How was Abraham "justified by works"; that is, how did his works demonstrate that he was righteous?

8. Verse 23: When was Abraham counted righteous by God?

9. Verse 26: To what does James compare faith without works?

DEVOTIONAL REFLECTIONS

1. How subtle and terrible sin is! Many of us by ourselves would not see how serious of a sin partiality or prejudice is. Even committing the smallest sin incurs the guilt of breaking the whole law of God. We should never make light of our sin, but say with David: "For thy name's sake, O LORD, pardon mine iniquity; for it is great" (Ps. 25:11).

2. In the middle of a very convicting chapter, James proclaims the glory of God's free grace, that God made a sovereign choice to save sinners (v. 5). God has chosen the foolish, the weak, the base, and the despised things of the world, an idolater like Abraham and an outcast like Rahab. In such light, no one is too sinful to be saved. Who might you think is the wickedest person you know? Pray for that person's conversion.

3. Just as money can be genuine or counterfeit, so, too, can faith be the real thing or just an imitation. Works cannot justify us before God, but they can and will demonstrate the genuineness of faith to the world. Martin Luther described it this way: "Oh, it is a living, busy, active, mighty thing, this faith; and so it is impossible for it not to do good works incessantly. It does not ask whether there are good works to do, but before the question rises, it has already done them, and is always at the doing of them. He who does not these works is a faithless man. He gropes and looks about after faith and good works, and knows neither what faith is nor what good works are, though he talks and talks, with many words, about faith and good works." Which kind of person are you?

Notes

1

2

3

4

5

6

7

8

Notes

9

10

11

12

13

14

15

Notes

16

17

18

STUDY QUESTIONS

1. Verse 1: Why shouldn't many people want to be teachers (KJV, masters)?

2. Verse 6: How is the tongue (our speech) like a fire?

3. Verses 7–8: How is the tongue more dangerous than wild animals?

4. Verse 13: How does a wise man show his wisdom?

5. Verses 14–15: What kind of wisdom produces envy and strife?

6. Verses 17–18: What are the characteristics of the wisdom that comes from God?

DEVOTIONAL REFLECTIONS

1. Small things show a lot about us. Like a skillful physician, James has tested our eyes for favoritism (2:1–13). Now he takes a close look at what our tongue tells us. What comes out of our mouths reveals what is in our hearts and what will happen to us on judgment day (Matt. 12:33–37). If you took stock of what your tongue produces over the course of a week, what would you learn about the health of your inner being?

2. We cannot by ourselves tame our tongues (v. 8). We need God to pardon us and renew us entirely. The so-called wisdom of man cannot help us. Only true wisdom can, the wisdom not found on earth but that comes down from heaven above. This wisdom comes from Christ, who through His Spirit and Word renews fallen image-bearers after His own image, and imparts to them a pure wisdom. How can we fill our minds and mouths with His wisdom?

Notes

1

2

3

4

5

6

7

Notes

8

9

10

11

12

13

14

Notes

15

16

17

STUDY QUESTIONS

1. Verse 2: What are common reasons why people fight and quarrel?

2. Verse 7: What must we do if we would overcome the devil?

3. Verse 10: What should we do if we want God to lift us up in honor and eternal reward?

4. Verse 12: Why is it wrong to judge other people?

5. Verses 14–15: How should we view our lives and our future?

6. Verse 17: Is sin only doing what is wrong? Why or why not?

DEVOTIONAL REFLECTIONS

1. Often in our minds, people are big and God is small. We strive with others while we depend little on God. How grateful we should be when God unmasks this as sin in our lives. Pray to see the fights and conflicts in your life as tools in His hand. Then confess to God any spiritual adultery of your heart.

2. James admonishes his readers to weep (vv. 9–10). While James is not saying that all forms of joy and laughter are wrong, he is saying that there is an important and prominent place for genuine, heartfelt repentance over all our sins. The psalmist says, "A broken and a contrite heart, O God, thou wilt not despise" (Ps. 51:17; see also 2 Cor. 7:10). Have you learned the grace of repentance?

3. Our attitudes toward the future are a good barometer of our hearts. When you think of later today, tomorrow, next year, and so on, is your disposition one that says "I will" or "If it is the Lord's will"? How will faith in God's providence affect your plans? Your prayers?

Notes

1

2

3

4

5

6

7

Notes

8

9

10

11

12

13

Notes

14

15

16

17

18

19

20

STUDY QUESTIONS

1. Verses 4–6: For what sins are these rich people rebuked?

2. Verses 7–8: How should the godly respond as they suffer injustice?

3. Verse 9: How should the coming of the Judge affect how we relate to each other?

4. Verse 13: How should a believer respond to hard times? To happy times?

5. Verse 16: What should believers do when they are sick?

6. Verses 17–18: How is Elijah (KJV, Elias) an example to us?

7. Verses 19–20: What is the joy of someone who helps someone else turn from sin to the Lord?

DEVOTIONAL REFLECTIONS

1. Christ's second coming is closer today than when James wrote these words. If Christ came today, would He find you living like verses 8–9 instruct us to live?

2. The church is a place where we should be able to bring our needs, petitions, joys, as well as our cares and concerns for others. Elders and ministers are particularly charged with the care of souls. James highlights their calling to the ministry of prayer. However, he calls all Christians to a life of continual prayer and praise (v. 13). How can you cultivate the practice of petition and thanksgiving in God's presence throughout your day?

3. Conversion involves saving a soul from death and hiding a multitude of sins (v. 20). Do you know this grace yourself? If not, you are still in your sins and heading toward death. Seek God's mercy in Jesus Christ. If you are converted, you will love to see others converted as well. Pray and seek for awakening and revival wherever God has placed you.

Introduction to the Book of
1 PETER

AUTHORSHIP: The author of this epistle was Simon Peter (1:1), the well-known and loved disciple of Christ, of whom we read in the Gospels and in the Acts of the Apostles. Both church history and internal evidence (5:1) within the epistle provide very strong evidence that 1 Peter was written by the apostle of Jesus. Evidently Peter's words were written down by Silvanus (or Silas), who was a traveling companion of Paul for some time (Acts 15:40) and, here, acted as Peter's scribe or amanuensis (1 Peter 5:12). That Peter was likely writing with an amanuensis may account for the more complex Greek that some suggest a lowly fisherman could not have written. The use of an amanuensis was not an uncommon feature of either New Testament material or other writings of the first century.

DATE: Peter is believed to have died in AD 67 in the persecutions of Nero, being hung upside down on a cross. We know from historical sources that persecution arising from anti-Christian sentiments grew strong in Rome around AD 64 during the reign of Nero (AD 54–68). Peter makes references to "Babylon" (5:13), which is likely a veiled reference to Rome. In view of the references to persecution and suffering in this epistle, it would seem probable that Peter wrote this letter to give comfort to suffering believers between the time of intense Christian suffering and his own death.

THEME: Hope through Christ in the midst of suffering.

PURPOSE: To encourage Christians to persevere in their suffering by setting before them the hope of grace reserved for them, as well as the glory of Jesus Christ.

SYNOPSIS
The Contribution of 1 Peter to Redemptive Revelation
Peter begins his epistle by lifting before the eyes of his readers the glorious privileges that they have through the gospel of Christ. The

church was in the midst of facing present and future trials, afflictions, and struggles. Peter reminds Christians that they are not alone because they are following in Christ's suffering and therefore that Christian suffering needs to be held within the context of God's love for His people, which began before the foundation of the world and will continue into glory. Christians suffer precisely because they are "strangers" and sojourners in this world. Christians experience suffering because they do not belong to this world and are to live lives that are contrary to the standards and ideals of this world; they are suffering for righteousness's sake (3:14). The Christian's time in this world is to be marked by cultivating a life of holiness (1:15), growing in grace and knowledge of God (2:2), shunning the "fleshly lusts, which war against the soul" (v. 11), and prayerfully awaiting "the end of all things" (4:7). In all their suffering, Christians are not to be "ashamed" but may confidently "commit the keeping" of their soul to God, "as unto a faithful Creator" (v. 19).

In this way Peter pursues his objective of pointing on the one hand to our glorious privileges and on the other hand to our duties as pilgrims, as husbands and wives, as sufferers for Christ's sake, as objects of this world's criticism and scorn—and yet, through it all, as heirs of glory. Every chapter, having looked at one problem or another of the believer's life in this world, ends with some vital uplifting truth. Chapter 1 ends with the inspiration of God's Word; chapter 2 with our soul's safety in Christ's care; chapter 3 with the reminder that Christ is now ascended with universal authority over all angels, as well as over all human authorities; chapter 4 with our souls in the care of a faithful Creator; and chapter 5 with the prayer that God will, after we have suffered a while in this world, make us perfect and bring us into his "eternal glory" (v. 10). The overall message is, "Look up!"

OUTLINE

I. Salutation (1:1–2)

II. Christian Characteristics (1:3–2:10)
    A. A Christian's Living Hope (1:3–12)
    B. A Christian's Holiness (1:13–25)
    C. A Christian's Sure Foundation (2:1–10)

Notes

1

2

3

4

5

6

Notes

7

8

9

10

11

Notes

12

13

14

15

16

17

Notes

18

19

20

21

22

23

Notes

24

25

STUDY QUESTIONS

1. Verses 1–2: How is each person in the Trinity involved in saving the people of God?

2. Verses 3–4: For what mercy does Peter bless God the Father?

3. Verses 6–7: How does Peter describe the trials that Christians endure?

4. Verses 10–11: What did God reveal to the ancient prophets?

5. Verses 14–17: How should God's holiness affect His children?

6. Verses 18–19: How were believers redeemed from the futile ways of their ancestors?

7. Verse 21: What is one purpose of Christ's resurrection and exaltation?

8. Verse 23: By what means does God cause people to be born again?

DEVOTIONAL REFLECTIONS

1. The struggle believers wage against sin is not because of anything in us but because of God's gracious plan in choosing whom He would save before the foundation of the world in eternity past. This is a great comfort to believers of all ages and reminds us that our struggle is not ours alone but rests in the sovereign and omnipotent plan of God (vv. 1–5). How can knowing God chose us encourage suffering believers?

2. Sometimes it is difficult to face the many trials and temptations of life. Peter tells us that the testing of our faith is so that it might be refined in the furnace of affliction. Much as gold is required to be heated and pressed and burned, so, too, must faith be tested. Yet the end result is that it proves itself true and genuine and precious (vv. 6–11).

3. Holiness and serious Christian living are not popular in this world, but they are our duty, required by God. God's demand that our lives be holy is not a stifling and burdensome requirement of His people. It is the gracious and loving call of God to His children to share in His holiness. In obeying, we show ourselves to be like our Father, who Himself is holy (vv. 12–25).

Notes

1

2

3

4

5

6

7

Notes

8

9

10

11

12

13

Notes

14

15

16

17

18

19

20

Notes

21

22

23

24

25

STUDY QUESTIONS

1. Verse 5: What are believers in Christ compared to?

2. Verse 6: What Scripture passage is quoted? What does it say about Christ?

3. Verse 9: What titles are given to the people of God? Why are they called by God?

4. Verses 13–14: How should believers treat civil officials?

5. Verse 15: What is one purpose for believers to conduct themselves this way?

6. Verse 17: What are our duties to different people?

7. Verse 21: What example did Christ leave for us to follow?

8. Verse 24: How does Christ's death affect the lives of His redeemed people?

DEVOTIONAL REFLECTIONS

1. There is no middle ground between Christ and holiness on the one side and the world and sin on the other. Yet the world's lies of wisdom, wealth, and pleasure can pose a real temptation for the Christian. It takes effort and concentration on a believer's part, as well as the grace of God, to reject the habits of his past life (vv. 1–3). But we must remember that no one can be indifferent to Christ. Either they will reverence Him or else they will reject His claims and His teaching (vv. 7–8).

2. Christ overcame the world by love and endurance of suffering, and so do Christians. The best way to silence critics of the gospel is to be full of good works. When a Christian is known only for his kindness, love, grace, and mercy, the world will try in vain to condemn him, and his righteous deeds will point unbelievers to the glory of God (vv. 11–20). When the Christian is called to suffer for his faith he should remind himself that he is only following in Christ's steps (vv. 21–25). How can that comfort the believer and give him endurance?

Notes

1

2

3

4

5

6

Notes

7

8

9

10

11

12

Notes

13

14

15

16

17

18

19

Notes

20

21

22

STUDY QUESTIONS

1. Verses 1–2: How should wives treat their husbands? How should the wives of men who disobey God seek to win their husbands?

2. Verse 7: What is the responsibility of husbands toward their wives?

3. Verse 9: How should believers respond when people mistreat them?

4. Verses 10–12: What Scripture passage is quoted here?

5. Verse 15: What should believers be prepared to do? How does that start with their attitude to the Lord?

6. Verse 18: What purpose of Christ's death is highlighted here?

7. Verse 22: What is Christ's position now?

DEVOTIONAL REFLECTIONS

1. The world idolizes physical beauty, but those who are wise prefer godliness in the heart (vv. 1–4). It is good to teach our children, even at a young age, that the beauty to admire in another is the inward beauty of a heart submissive to God.

2. It is biblical to teach that the man is the head of the home (1 Cor. 11:3; Eph. 5:23). He must not abuse his authority but pair it with a Christlike spirit of self-sacrifice (Eph. 5:25–29). Peter admonishes husbands here to live with their wives in understanding. Submission need not be a negative thing when properly carried out (1 Peter 3:5–9).

3. Pilgrims who are on a journey are to have their lives characterized by a heavenly standard. Christians ought not to be concerned with winning the approval of a worldly standard on which they have turned their backs. Rather, Christians ought to be concerned with doing what pleases God and therefore to have His blessing (vv. 10–17).

4. The Bible does not teach that we are automatically saved by the sacraments of baptism and the Lord's Supper. On the contrary, in order to be saved we must be born again, as Christ teaches (John 3:1–8). But the sacraments have their own place in church life as seals and confirmations of the promises of God (1 Peter 3:18–22).

Notes

1

2

3

4

5

6

7

Notes

8

9

10

11

12

13

Notes

14

15

16

17

18

19

STUDY QUESTIONS

1. Verses 3–4: What sins did these believers once commit? How did their unbelieving friends react to their conversion?

2. Verse 7: What should motivate Christians to be sober, watchful, and frequent in prayer?

3. Verses 10–11: What does Peter teach about spiritual gifts and their use?

4. Verse 13: Why should believers rejoice when they suffer for being Christians?

5. Verse 14: What privilege do believers enjoy when they are insulted for Christ's sake?

6. Verse 19: What should believers do when they suffer for doing God's will (1 Peter 2:23)?

DEVOTIONAL REFLECTIONS

1. The difference made in anyone who is born again is that rebirth reverses his whole moral outlook. He now loves what before he hated and now hates what before he loved. So great a change is made in one who is truly converted that it may amaze his friends and neighbors (vv. 1–6). Has God changed you on the inside? How?

2. If God has given us a gift to edify our fellow believers, we ought not to neglect it but use it. However, we must never attempt to serve God by following and teaching our own wisdom in place of His Word. And we would be fools to try to minister in our own strength instead of in the strength God supplies by His Spirit. This is the way to glorify God, for serving by the Word and Spirit is serving by faith in Christ (vv. 7–11).

3. Worldly men have little conception of what awaits them in the day of death when they must appear before the holy God. On the other hand, those who believe in God's holiness and the judgment day should not be surprised when God sends fiery trials to purify them, including the fire of persecution. Instead, let Christians live so that if men attack them, it will not be for their sins but for their sincere obedience to God (vv. 12–19).

Notes

1

2

3

4

5

6

7

Notes

8

9

10

11

12

Notes

13

14

1. Verses 2–3: What is the duty of elders? How should they do that duty?

2. Verse 4: What hope belongs to faithful elders?

3. Verse 7: How should believers handle their cares and anxieties?

4. Verse 10: What will God do after we have suffered in this brief life?

5. Verse 13: Who is Mark (KJV, Marcus; see Acts 12:12, 25; 13:13; 15:37–39; Col. 4:10; 2 Tim. 4:11; Philemon 24)?

DEVOTIONAL REFLECTIONS

1. Those who bear an office or position of authority in God's church must be careful not to become "lords over God's heritage" (v. 3). Wherever there are positions of authority, the sinful heart is tempted to be puffed up with pride and self-centeredness. On the other hand, it is easy for leaders to lose their eagerness and readiness to serve in anticipation of Christ's reward (vv. 1–4). How can knowing that Christ will return in glory help leaders to guard themselves from both arrogance and laziness?

2. Augustine once said that if he were asked the most important three qualities of the Christian life, he would say, "Humility, humility, humility." God hates pride and warns against it but tenderly cares for the humble in all their anxieties (vv. 5–7). How can we clothe ourselves in humility every day?

Introduction to the Book of
2 PETER

AUTHORSHIP: The author of this epistle is Simon Peter, the disciple and apostle of the Lord Jesus Christ. Many scholars have expressed either difficulty with or flat out rejection of the Petrine authorship of 2 Peter. They argue: (1) this epistle uses very different language than 1 Peter, including many Greek words used nowhere else in Scripture; (2) it was written after Paul's letters were recognized as Scripture and collected (2 Peter 3:15–16); (3) it looks back to the apostles and early Christians as a previous generation that has already died (vv. 2, 4); (4) an apostle would never have copied the writing of another writer, as, some argue, 2 Peter does with Jude.

In reply to these arguments, we may say: (1) Peter may have written his epistles with different secretaries (1 Peter 5:12), who, under the inspiration of the Holy Spirit (2 Peter 1:20–21), could have significantly shaped the style of each letter; (2) the reference to Paul and putting "all his epistles" on the same level as "the other scriptures" (3:15–16) implies only that the author knew of some epistles from Paul, and recognized, as Paul did, that the apostolic writings are the authoritative Word of God (v. 2; 1 Cor. 2:13; 14:37; 2 Thess. 3:14); (3) "the fathers" who had died are not the apostolic generation, but previous generations of Israelites extending back to the patriarchs (2 Peter 3:4).

As to the relationship between 2 Peter 2–3 and Jude (argument 4), it is not clear which was the original, or if both draw from another source. Though similar, they are far from exact copies in the Greek text. In any case, the apostles could have either arrived at similar thoughts independently or felt free to draw upon materials that were true and trustworthy. We observe similar parallels between portions of Kings, Chronicles, Isaiah, and Jeremiah, and between the Gospels. Therefore the arguments against Peter's authorship are not convincing.

The epistle clearly testifies that Peter is the author. (1) The author wrote as "Simon Peter, a servant and an apostle of Jesus Christ" (1:1). (2) He was a witness to Christ's transfiguration (vv. 16–18). (3) He was familiar with the epistles of Paul, whom he refers affectionately to as "our beloved brother" (3:15). (4) He was obviously very familiar with the Old Testament. (5) He informs us that this is his "second epistle" (v. 1). Unlike other (apocryphal) writings falsely bearing Peter's name, this epistle teaches no false doctrine. The church has long accepted it as an authentic writing of the apostle, recognizing the divinely inspired quality of its words.

DATE: Dating the epistle depends on Peter's remark of his coming martyrdom (1:14–15). Church tradition indicates that Peter was killed under the reign of Emperor Nero, being crucified upside down. Therefore, 2 Peter was written near the end of Peter's life (c. AD 64–67). Second Peter was likely written from Rome even as his first epistle was ("Babylon," 1 Peter 5:13). It is probable that the recipients of 2 Peter, though not identified, were the same as those of his first epistle (2 Peter 3:1)—elect Christians who were living in Asia Minor (1 Peter 1:1–2).

THEME: The necessity of spiritual growth and the danger of false teaching.

PURPOSE: To call Christians to persevere and flourish in apostolic Christianity, and to warn them of the deceptive nature of false teachers who had crept in to lead the people of God astray.

SYNOPSIS
The Contribution of 2 Peter to Redemptive Revelation
Peter summed up the twin message of this epistle in its last two verses: beware of being led astray by sinful and false teachers (3:17; expounded in chs. 2–3), and grow in the grace and knowledge of the Lord (3:18; expounded in ch. 1). He had evidently heard that false teachers had infiltrated the churches and were spreading their harmful influence among the Lord's people. Wishing to put his readers on guard against theological error propagated by false prophets and false teachers (2:1), Peter warns them against their errors. The false doctrines of these men centered on the denial of the judgment. Peter not only defends the judgment but pronounces fearful judgment upon all false teachers. Peter manifests a zeal for truth, exhorting his readers to believe nothing but the inspired Word of God, which he calls "a light that shineth in a dark place" (1:19). The way of guarding against such heresies is to revel in the Scriptures, which alone are sufficient to reveal to us the true nature of God. They also reveal what God requires from man and

promises to him, both of which will be fulfilled in the day of the Lord. Thus Peter urges God's people on to full maturity and to due diligence in regard to one's salvation.

OUTLINE
I. Salutation (1:1)

II. Encouragement to Press On in the Christian Faith (1:2–21)
    A. Blessing of Increasing Grace through God's Promises (1:2–4)
    B. Call to Grow in Every Grace unto Assurance (1:5–11)
    C. Reminder in View of Peter's Imminent Death (1:12–15)
    D. Testimony to Christ's Transfiguration Glory (1:16–18)
    E. The Illuminating and Sure Word of Scripture (1:19–21)

III. Warning against False Teachers (2:1–3:16)
    A. Description of False Teachers (2:1–3)
    B. Illustrations of Their Destruction (2:4–9)
    C. Corruption of False Teachers (2:10–22)
    D. Exhortation to Remember Prophetic and Apostolic Teaching (3:1–2)
    E. Objection of the Scoffers against Christ's Coming (3:3–9)
    F. Expectation of the Day of the Lord (3:10–13)
    G. Application by Diligence and Faithfulness to Scripture (3:14–16)

IV. Concluding Command to Avoid Error and Grow in Grace (3:17–18)

Notes

1

2

3

4

5

Notes

6

7

8

9

10

11

12

Notes

13

14

15

16

17

18

19

Notes

20

21

STUDY QUESTIONS

1. Verse 3: What has God given to believers? Through what means did He give it (v. 2)?

2. Verses 5–7: In what areas should believers strive to grow?

3. Verses 8–9: What can a lack of spiritual growth do to a believer?

4. Verses 10–11: What will growth in these areas do for a believer?

5. Verse 14: What did Peter anticipate would happen to him soon?

6. Verses 16–18: Of what event was Peter an eyewitness (Mark 9:1–8)? How does he describe it?

7. Verses 20–21: How were the prophetic messages of the Holy Scriptures written?

DEVOTIONAL REFLECTIONS

1. Sanctification, unlike justification, is a lifelong process. To bear fruit believers must give all diligence to add every virtue to the knowledge they possess. The diligent Christian will by his life enjoy confirmation of his election in this life. The biblical doctrine of election does not promote laziness, but holiness. John Calvin said, "Purity of life is not improperly called the evidence and proof of election." After this life the faithful believer will enjoy a royal reception when he gets home to glory. In what areas of sanctification do you especially need to grow? Has spiritual growth in the past confirmed your sense that you belong to Christ and are headed for glory? If so, how? If not, why not?

2. The faithful teaching and life of those who have discipled us will be remembered with love long after they have gone home (Heb. 13:7). We should all seek to leave behind a legacy of truth. Will you be remembered as one who faithfully shared with others the truths of Scripture?

3. The record of Christ's life and miracles is no fabled invention but is absolutely reliable and solid truth. The world is a dark place full of idolatry, vain philosophy, and crime, but the Bible is the one sure light that points out the path to heaven. Read it and love it.

Notes

1

2

3

4

5

6

Notes

7

8

9

10

11

12

13

14

15

16

17

18

Notes

19

20

21

22

STUDY QUESTIONS

1. Verse 1: Against whom must Christians be on guard?

2. Verses 4–6: What are some examples of God's judgment on the wicked?

3. Verse 9: What can we learn from the experiences of Noah (v. 5) and Lot (v. 7)?

4. Verses 12–14: How does Peter describe these false teachers?

5. Verse 17: What do these images imply about the false teachers?

6. Verse 19: What do these false teachers promise people? What is the truth of the matter?

7. Verse 22: What does the saying about a dog and a pig imply about people who fell away?

DEVOTIONAL REFLECTIONS

1. History bears eloquent testimony to the truth of what Peter says here concerning the danger of teachers of false religion. Yet in this age of so-called tolerance, Christians are often afraid to exercise discernment and to speak against heresy. Our silence is wrong, because all error corrupts, and errors against the foundations of the faith destroy souls forever. What damnable heresies presently endanger the Christian church? Pray for boldness for yourself and preachers to speak against them for the sake of precious souls.

2. The Old Testament proves repeatedly that God will destroy the wicked, especially those who lead others into wickedness like the false prophets. In their arrogance and boasting, they may appear successful and happy. However, unregenerate preachers are walking on a tightrope, and if they do not repent and find salvation, they will plunge at last into the fire of hell. We must remind ourselves of the danger into which we put ourselves if we listen to them. Regardless of the popularity of a preacher or teacher, do not give him a voice in your life, family, or church unless he speaks the truth of the Word of God and lives that truth with integrity.

Notes

Chapter 3

1

2

3

4

5

6

7

Notes

8

9

10

11

12

Notes

13

14

15

16

17

18

STUDY QUESTIONS

1. Verses 3–4: What did Peter predict people would say about Christ's second coming?

2. Verses 8–9: What should we remember when considering how long the church has waited for Christ's return?

3. Verse 10: What will take place on the day of the Lord?

4. Verse 13: What has God promised to make for His people?

5. Verses 15–16: What does Peter say about Paul's letters?

6. Verse 18: What should be the goal of God's children?

DEVOTIONAL REFLECTIONS

1. Peter's warning about scoffers is fulfilled in our own day in that many have been seduced away from the Christian faith by the theory of evolution and skepticism regarding the worldwide flood. Just as Christians in the early church were tempted to compromise and distort aspects of biblical truth to fit into Jewish traditions and Greek philosophies, so, too, Christians today are tempted to do the same to fit our faith into modern and postmodern philosophies. Removing Christianity from the realms of real history and science destroys the faith. It is for the well-being of our own souls and that of our fellow believers that we reject all theories about the origin and destiny of the world which conflict with biblical teaching. How do you encounter this pressure, and how can you arm yourself against it?

2. The day of the Lord is coming. The elements will burn in the fire of God's judgment, and a new creation will arise where righteousness dwells and sin has no place. Nothing will last except Christ and obedience to His Word. On the one hand, this calls us to forcefully reject all heresies, removing false teachers from the church. On the other hand, this demands that we seek first the kingdom of God and His righteousness, making it our great priority to gain and grow in our knowledge of Christ and likeness to Him. Standing against doctrinal error and running after spiritual growth are not mere options, much less distractions, for the Christian. They are the very essence of being a people who hope in Christ alone. How could you better live in light of eternity?

Introduction to the Book of
1 JOHN

AUTHORSHIP: The text of this epistle does not bear the author's name, nor greetings common to the epistles, yet it is evidently the work of the apostle John. He claims to be an eyewitness of Christ, preaching to others the Savior he saw, touched, and heard (1:1–3; 4:14). He declares a message which he received from God (1:5). He writes as a spiritual father, addressing all his readers affectionately as "my little children" (2:1), just as the apostle Paul did (Gal. 4:19). He writes with great authority, for to refuse to listen to him shows that a person does not know God (1 John 4:6). Thus the author places himself in the circle of the apostles, men appointed by Christ to be His witnesses and authoritative spokesmen. The style and vocabulary of this epistle are remarkably similar to those of the gospel of John, which is why we may conclude that John is the author of this epistle as well. Polycarp (d. c. AD 155), a student of John, cites this epistle, and Irenaeus (d. AD 202), a student of Polycarp, attributes it to the apostle John.

DATE: Uncertain; if written after the gospel of John, then perhaps AD 85–95. Clement of Rome appears to cite the book around AD 96.

THEME: Personal assurance of genuine salvation.

PURPOSE: To clarify the difference between those who belong to God and those who belong to this world so that the church may enjoy peace and joy in Christ.

SYNOPSIS

The Contribution of 1 John to Redemptive Revelation
John does not name a church or region to which he writes. With Peter, the apostle to the Jews, John was a pillar of the church in Jerusalem (Acts 3:1; 4:13, 19; 8:14; Gal. 2:8–9). Tradition locates his ministry in Ephesus after the destruction of Jerusalem in AD 70. It may be that he wrote predominantly to Jewish believers, for he says they had known

God's commandment "from the beginning," a time frame reaching back to Genesis (1 John 1:1; 2:7, 13–14; 3:8, 11–12).

John's epistle addresses a situation where false teachers denied that the man Jesus was the Christ (2:22; 4:1–3; John 1:14). In Greek thinking, a spiritual being such as Christ could not become flesh. This may be the heresy of Docetism, which taught that Christ appeared human but in fact was a spirit. The false teachers may also have taught an early form of Gnosticism, for Irenaeus said that John wrote his Gospel against the heresy of Cerinthus, who claimed that the Christ-Spirit came upon Jesus at baptism but left prior to the crucifixion. Such a divorce of spirit and body often implied that the acts of the body do not affect spiritual life; thus John stresses righteous conduct to counteract these false teachings. Though at first working in the church, the false teachers eventually broke away to form their own movement (1 John 2:18–19). This disruption in the church no doubt shook the confidence of the remaining believers.

John responded to this crisis by writing a pastoral letter that drew a simple yet profound picture of the difference between the children of God and the people of this world. The letter contains a series of stark contrasts: life versus death (1:1–2; 2:25; 3:14–16; 5:11–13, 16–17, 20), light versus darkness (1:5–7; 2:8–11), truth versus lies (1:6, 8; 2:4, 8, 21–22, 27; 3:7, 18–19; 4:1, 6; 5:6, 20), righteousness and keeping God's commandments versus sin (2:3–4, 7–8, 29; 3:3–10, 22–24; 4:21–5:3), and love versus hate (2:9–11; 3:10–18, 23; 4:7–12, 16–21; 5:1–3).

John's message centers on God's nature as light and love (1:5; 4:8, 16), revealed in the person and work of His Son. Jesus is both the Son of God and God Himself (5:20). He came in the flesh, as a real man who could be seen and touched (1:1; 4:2). The Father sent His Son into the world to give life to sinners (1:2; 4:9, 14; 5:11–12), though the world hates God (3:13; 4:10). With Christ's incarnation, God's light shone into the darkness (2:8), and His love was displayed (4:9). Christ brought a message about God (1:5) and exemplified that message in His own sinless life (2:1, 6, 29; 3:5, 7). He died as the propitiation for sins (2:2; 4:10) to make His people completely clean and forgiven (1:7, 9; 2:12), and now He lives to intercede for His people as their heavenly Advocate when they sin (v. 1). He causes blind sinners to know the true God (5:20) as the Spirit bears witness within them so they know the truth of Christ (2:20, 27; 4:2, 6; 5:6, 10). Christ has power to conquer the devil and destroy sin in those united to Himself by faith (3:5–9; 5:5) as the

Spirit dwells in them (3:24; 4:12–13). One day, Christ will come in glory so that the wicked will be ashamed (2:28) and God's children will see Him as He is (3:2).

John uses three expressions—"born of God," "abiding in him," and "knowing him"—to describe how God applies the work of Christ to the individual sinner. In the new birth, God produces a new nature inclined to faith, love, and righteous activity (2:29; 3:8–9; 4:7; 5:1, 4, 18). The implanting of gospel truth in the regenerated soul causes him to no longer deny his sinfulness but confess his sins to God (1:8–10). God the Father makes him into His child and a stranger to this world (3:1), which is ruled by the devil (vv. 9–10).

The Christian life is a life of "abiding"—entering and remaining in spiritual union with Jesus Christ (2:6, 10, 17). His Word and the anointing of the Spirit abide within the soul (vv. 14, 24, 27; 3:9) so that he dwells in union with God (4:15–16). God's life and love abide in the believer, transforming his soul (2:28–29; 3:6, 15, 17, 24; 4:11–13). The believer abides in the true church (2:19), and enjoys fellowship with God, Christ, and all who walk in the light (1:3, 7).

However, God's child still sins (1:8–2:1) and possesses a varying degree of maturity (2:12–14). He must resist the alluring idols of this world and live for eternity (vv. 15–17; 5:21), purifying himself of sin (3:3), and following in the self-denying, others-serving footsteps of Jesus (2:6; 3:18). Only when Christ returns will the Christian reach total Christlikeness (v. 2).

Abiding in Him is not merely a mystical experience; it also involves spiritual knowledge. John repeatedly writes of "knowing" the Lord in a way unique to believers (2:3–4, 13–14, 29; 3:1, 6; 4:6, 7–8; 5:20). This knowledge includes doctrinal understanding and discernment (2:18, 20–21; 3:2, 5, 15–16; 4:2, 6, 16; 5:18, 20), and yet it is an experiential knowledge with practical results (2:3–4; 3:6; 4:7–8). Spiritual knowledge culminates in personal assurance that we know God and are united with Him in Christ (2:3, 5, 28–29; 3:14–15, 19, 24; 4:13; 5:2, 13, 15, 19–20).

Thus John presents a vivid picture of authentic Christianity so that believers can know they are the children of God, united to His Son, and possessors of life—to their great joy (1:4; 5:13).

OUTLINE

John's first epistle is difficult to outline because of his fluid and cyclic style. At least a dozen different outlines have been proposed by scholars. The following outline notes a cycle in the first main section of two contrasts and then a promise, repeated four times (1:5–3:24). The second section focuses on exhortations and motives (4:1–5:17). Both sections end on a note of confidence or boldness toward God in prayer (3:21; 5:14).

I. Incarnation of the Word of Life (1:1–4)

II. Contrast between God's True Children and the World (1:5–3:24)
   A. Walking with God in Gospel Forgiveness (1:5–2:2)
      1. Contrast: Fellowship with Light or Darkness (1:5–7)
      2. Contrast: Confession of Sin or Self-Deception (1:8–10)
      3. Promise of Christ's Propitiation and Intercession (2:1–2)
   B. Obeying God's Law of Love in Gospel Privileges (2:3–14)
      1. Contrast: Obedience or Disobedience to His Commandments (2:3–6)
      2. Contrast: Love in the Light or Hate in the Darkness (2:7–11)
      3. Promises to Children, Young Men, and Fathers (2:12–14)
   C. Resisting Temptation in Gospel Hope (2:15–3:3)
      1. Contrast: Love of the Father or Love of the World (2:15–17)
      2. Contrast: Christ-Centered Truth or Anti-Christian Lies (2:18–27)
      3. Promise of His Coming for God's Children (2:28–3:3)
   D. Doing Righteousness and Love with Gospel Boldness (3:4–24)
      1. Contrast: Righteousness by Christ or Sin by the Devil (3:4–10)
      2. Contrast: Love and Life or Hatred and Death (3:11–18)
      3. Promise of Confidence toward God (3:19–24)

III. Exhortations and Motives to Abide in God's Truth and Love (4:1–5:17)
   A. Do Not Trust False Prophets (4:1–6)
   B. Love One Another (4:7–5:3)
      1. God's Love in God's Son (4:7–10)
      2. God's Love in God's Children (4:11–21)
      3. Loving Brothers and Obeying God (5:1–3)
   C. Hold Onto the Witness to Christ by Faith (5:4–13)
   D. Pray with Confidence for Each Other (5:14–17)

IV. Conclusion (5:18–21)
   A. Knowledge Is in Christ (5:18–20)
   B. Watch against Idols (5:21)

Notes

1

2

3

4

5

6

7

Notes

8

9

10

STUDY QUESTIONS

1. Verses 1–2: In what way did eternal life come to man? What does this have to do with Jesus?

2. Verses 3–4: What are some of John's purposes in this letter?

3. Verse 5: What do we learn about God? What does that mean?

4. Verse 7: How is it possible for sinners to have fellowship with God?

5. Verses 9–10: What is one difference between Christians and non-Christians?

DEVOTIONAL REFLECTIONS

1. It was stunning and virtually inconceivable to the ancient Greek mind that the divine Word would become a physical man we could see and touch. It should be stunning to us today that the Lord Jesus would take our lowly nature to His glorious person. Life has come to us in a way we can relate to, with gentleness and sympathy for our weaknesses. Consider these truths and spend some time praising God for what He did for sinners. How can Christians who lack joy in Christ acquire more genuine joy? What role does the Holy Spirit play in helping true believers experience fullness of joy?

2. A relationship with the righteous God cannot coexist happily with sin. We must not call ourselves Christians and walk in the darkness; we must walk in the light, allowing Christ to expose our sin, wash us clean, and lead us in His ways. How often do you confess your sins to God? How do you use the Word to help you to see, hate, and forsake sin?

Notes

1

2

3

4

5

6

7

8

Notes

9

10

11

12

13

14

Notes

15

16

17

18

19

20

21

Notes

22

23

24

25

26

27

Notes

28

29

STUDY QUESTIONS

1. Verses 1–2: How is Christ the complete remedy for sin?

2. Verse 3: How can we know that we know Christ?

3. Verse 6: What is the mark of someone who abides in the Lord?

4. Verses 10–11: What is another mark of someone who walks in the light of God?

5. Verses 15–17: What characterizes the world and its love?

6. Verse 18: Who will come? Who has already come, even in John's day?

7. Verses 20–21: What do Christians have so that they know God's truth?

8. Verse 23: What is true about someone who denies that Jesus is God's Son?

9. Verse 28: What will those who abide in the Lord have when He comes?

10. Verse 29: What is one evidence of being born of God?

DEVOTIONAL REFLECTIONS

1. Sometimes when we take our children to a park, we pay for their admission and their hands get stamped to show that their admission price has been paid. John explains the stamp that marks those who truly know God: they obey God's laws, love God's people, and receive God's doctrines. They should remember, however, that these marks did not pay for their admission to the kingdom; only the death and intercession of God's righteous Son does so. How can the marks and payment of salvation guide a person doubting his salvation?

2. Why is it important to fight against sin? How can we go on fighting against sin without becoming discouraged by our numerous failures? What comfort do true believers find in Jesus's work as their advocate when they do sin and repent of it?

3. God's people have the anointing of the Spirit to teach them the truth. Their faith does not depend on human testimony or secret knowledge from a special teacher, but on God's Spirit speaking through God's Word (1 Cor. 2:1–5). However, God's Spirit does work through Bible teachers (John 21:15; Eph. 4:11). How should we give due respect and attention to teachers without giving them the place of the Spirit?

Notes

1

2

3

4

5

6

7

Notes

8

9

10

11

12

13

14

Notes

15

16

17

18

19

20

21

22

Notes

23

24

STUDY QUESTIONS

1. Verses 1–2: What is one way that God has shown His marvelous love for His own? What will this mean for them when He comes?

2. Verse 4: What is sin?

3. Verses 8–10: What two groups are named here? What is the difference between them?

4. Verse 12: What did Cain do (Gen. 4:1–12)? Why? What does that show about him?

5. Verse 15: What does hatred reveal?

6. Verses 16–18: What does genuine love require?

7. Verse 19: How can we find assurance of salvation?

8. Verse 23: What is John's summary of what God commands?

DEVOTIONAL REFLECTIONS

1. This chapter contrasts God's children and the world in terms of righteousness versus sin, love versus hatred, and life versus death. How would you summarize the difference between a true Christian and an unsaved person? Where do you stand?

2. If we are true believers, how does a proper understanding of the doctrine of adoption impact our relationship with God as our Father (v. 1)? With the world (v. 1)? With the future (v. 2)? With ourselves (v. 3)? With the family of believers (vv. 14–18)?

3. If you are born of God, then God has given you promises. When Christ comes, you will gaze into His glory without shame and be made like Him. You can have confidence toward God right now because the Spirit is working in your life. Do you have a right to claim these promises? Which of these promises is most precious to you now, and why?

Notes

1

2

3

4

5

6

Notes

7

8

9

10

11

12

13

14

Notes

15

16

17

18

19

20

21

STUDY QUESTIONS

1. Verses 2–3: What is an important test of whether a message is from God's Spirit?

2. Verse 6: What did the apostle John say was a test of whether a person knows God?

3. Verses 9–10: How did God demonstrate His love? What does this show us about Him?

4. Verse 12: How does the invisible God dwell within His children?

5. Verse 15: What is required for God to dwell in us?

6. Verse 18: What can God's love do to the fear of punishment in our hearts?

7. Verse 19: Why do we love God?

DEVOTIONAL REFLECTIONS

1. What false teachers present themselves to us today in person or through media? How can you recognize them? (See v. 2; Deut. 13:1–3; Matt. 7:15–20; Acts 17:10–12; Gal. 1:8–9; 1 Tim. 4:1–5.) How should you respond? How do the differences between those who are of the world and those who are of God affect your daily life and relationships? Should they affect you and your family more? In what ways?

2. God is love; as the Puritans said, Christ is love covered over with flesh. The Christian life is the indwelling of God's love in men, women, and children. Christ's coming aims to produce peace and joy in His beloved, not terror. How prominent is love in your view of God? Is His love hidden behind His majesty or wrath? How can you meditate more on His love? How can you grow in your own practice of Christlike love?

Notes

1

2

3

4

5

6

7

8

Notes

9

10

11

12

13

14

15

Notes

16

17

18

19

20

21

1. Verse 1: What is another evidence of having been born of God?

2. Verses 4–5: What does faith in Christ enable a believer to do?

3. Verses 11–12: What is God's testimony concerning His Son?

4. Verse 13: What was one of John's purposes in writing this letter?

5. Verse 16: What should a Christian do if he sees another Christian sinning?

6. Verse 20: What does John teach here about Christ and His work?

7. Verse 21: With what warning does John close his letter?

DEVOTIONAL REFLECTIONS

1. Christ is the teacher of His people by His Word and Spirit. He gives us the truth and convinces us of its validity by divine and authoritative testimony in the Word and in the heart. The triune God is Himself the witness to this truth. Therefore, we should submit to the Bible and receive all that it says, regardless of what men may say.

2. Consider what it means to overcome the world (vv. 4–5). Why is it necessary to engage in spiritual warfare in order to overcome the world? In what ways can we rise above the world's way of thinking and resist worldly peer pressure? Who gives us the power to do that? Offer an example from your own life of overcoming the world by the Spirit's grace.

3. God wants His children to know that they have life. He does not delight in slavish fear among believers but in their assurance. Based on what you have read in this book, how can someone have assurance of being God's child? How can one grow in that assurance?

Introduction to the Book of
2 JOHN

AUTHORSHIP: The author identifies himself simply as "the elder," but the style and teachings of this epistle link it (and the third epistle) closely to John's first epistle (see Introduction to 1 John). An apostle could refer to himself as an elder, for Peter did so (1 Peter 5:1). Irenaeus (d. AD 202) quotes 2 John and ascribes it to John, the disciple of the Lord. Thus we may conclude that it was written by the apostle John.

DATE: Uncertain. This epistle appears to address the same crisis as 1 John (2 John 7; 1 John 2:18–27) and thus may have been written around the same time, perhaps AD 85–95.

THEME: The importance of love and truth for the church of the elect.

PURPOSE: To lovingly exhort a church and its members to watch that they continue in love and the truth of Christ though false teachers have appeared.

SYNOPSIS

The Contribution of 2 John to Redemptive Revelation
John's second letter addresses "the elect lady and her children," which, given that Israel (Isa. 52:2), the church (Rev. 21:9), and ancient cities (Isa. 47:1) were often addressed as women, likely refers to a church and its members. He shows them that the Christian life consists of both truth and love (2 John 3). God's truth commands us to love one another (v. 5), and enters the soul to produce that love (v. 1). Love makes Christian leaders rejoice to hear that people are faithfully living in submission to the truth (v. 4). Love especially moves Christians to rejoice in being together with other faithful people (v. 12). Yet, John warns, love does not encourage us to welcome every teacher but to remain faithful to the ancient truth revealed by God (v. 6). Churches must discern those who fundamentally reject God's truth about Christ (v. 7), staying alert for they threaten their eternal well-being (v. 8). Teachers who do not receive the truth of Christ are outsiders to God and His church

and should receive no welcome or encouragement from the people of God (vv. 10–11).

OUTLINE
I. Greetings in Truth and Love (vv. 1–3)
II. Commendation for Walking in Love (vv. 4–6)
III. Warning against False Teachers (vv. 7–11)
IV. Conclusion and Greetings (vv. 12–13)

Notes

1

2

3

4

5

6

Notes

7

8

9

10

11

12

13

STUDY QUESTIONS

1. Verses 1–2: What does John say about truth, love, and God's people?

2. Verse 6: What defines what it means to love one another?

3. Verse 7: What shows that a teacher is a deceiver and an antichrist?

4. Verses 10–11: What should Christians not do for false teachers?

5. Verse 12: How would John prefer to communicate with these people? Why?

DEVOTIONAL REFLECTIONS

1. Truth and love are closely related to each other. What are the consequences of having truth without love? Love without truth? What does it mean to love someone "in the truth" (v. 1)? How can we improve the balance of truth and love in our relationships at home, at church, at school, and in society?

2. The truth of Christ creates love in the family of God. Why is this so? Why is it that those who trust in God's truth find themselves attracted to each other and desiring to serve one another?

3. Christians must give no approval or support to false teachers. Those who seek to publicly promote lies contrary to fundamental truths about Christ are not misguided brothers but deadly enemies. Christians should love them, pray for them, and try to show them their errors. But believers should not offer them the least encouragement or hospitality, for this gives false teachers an open door to spread their soul-damning errors.

Introduction to the Book of
3 JOHN

AUTHORSHIP: The apostle John. See Introduction to 2 John: Authorship.

DATE: Uncertain; probably late in the first century.

THEME: Love for the truth and support for true Christian teachers.

PURPOSE: To encourage love among brothers and service to traveling missionaries.

SYNOPSIS

The Contribution of 3 John to Redemptive Revelation

John wrote this letter to a faithful Christian man about whom we know little except his name, Gaius. This common Latin name belonged to other men in the New Testament (Acts 19:29; 20:4; Rom. 16:23; 1 Cor. 1:14)—and to more than one Roman dictator. The Gaius whom John loved was no dictator. John calls him "beloved" four times in this short epistle (3 John 1, 2, 5, 11), a lavish reminder of his pleasure in Gaius's faithfulness. He is a model of soul prosperity (v. 2) by the power of God's truth (vv. 3–4), producing the fruit of love and missionary support (vv. 5–8).

In contrast stands Diotrephes, a leader in a local church. Whereas true servants of the Lord seek the glory of His name through the gospel (v. 7), Diotrephes sought his own glory (v. 9). It does not appear that he was a heretic, for John makes no mention of false doctrine here. Yet despite his orthodoxy the truth had not entered his heart, and his proud and divisive conduct implied that he did not belong to God (v. 11). He slandered the broader church and refused to allow anyone in his congregation to welcome missionaries as they traveled through the area (v. 10).

Where John's second epistle warns against welcoming false teachers, the third gives a balancing exhortation for believers to warmly receive and help preachers who seek the glory of Christ and to maintain fellowship with other congregations.

OUTLINE

I. Greeting: Love in the Truth (v. 1)
II. Blessing and Joy in Gaius (vv. 2–4)
III. Commendation for Caring for Missionaries (vv. 5–8)
IV. Warning against Diotrephes (vv. 9–11)
V. Conclusion and Greeting (vv. 12–14)

Notes

1

2

3

4

5

6

7

8

Notes

9

10

11

12

13

14

15

STUDY QUESTIONS

1. Verse 4: What gave John great joy? What does that show about a true spiritual leader?

2. Verses 5–6: What should churches do for visiting missionaries and Bible teachers?

3. Verses 7–8: What motivates faithful missionaries and teachers? What does not motivate them?

4. Verses 9–10: For what sins does John criticize Diotrephes? Why did Diotrephes act that way?

5. Verse 11: What do people's actions show about their relationship with God?

DEVOTIONAL REFLECTIONS

1. How is Gaius a good example for us to follow? What does it mean to "walk in truth" (v. 4)? How could we and our families walk in the truth more effectively?

2. William Carey, pioneer missionary to India, once compared missions to descending into a deep mine to recover treasures, and said, "I will go down, but you must hold the ropes." Missionaries need the support of other Christians. This epistle makes it clear that they need not only financial assistance but also love and hospitality. How do you share your resources, love, and home to strengthen those who go out to the nations for the Lord's sake?

3 It is easy to point the finger at arrogant leaders like Diotrephes who try to take Christ's place, but we must begin with our own pride. John Newton said, "I have read of many wicked popes, but the worst pope I ever met is Pope Self." How do you see Diotrephes's pride operating in yourself? How can you combat it? Demetrius was spoken well of by all men (v. 12). What would those who know us best say about our love for the truth and for hospitality? What would our non-Christian neighbors say?

Introduction to the Book of
JUDE

AUTHORSHIP: The letter was written by Jude, the "brother of James" (v. 1). While the name *Jude* (Hebrew: *Judah*, Greek: *Judas*) was very common (Luke 6:16), scholarship identifies this particular Jude as Jesus's half brother. The James mentioned in Jude 1 is most likely the well-known leader of the church in Jerusalem (Acts 15:13) who was another half brother of Jesus (Gal. 1:19; cf. Matt. 13:55; Mark 6:3; James 1:1). Jude's greeting and teaching are similar to James's, and Jude does not include himself within the original group of apostles (Jude 17–18).

DATE: Jude wrote this letter between AD 55–80, most likely in the mid-60s. Church historian Eusebius records that Jude and his son had already died by AD 81. Jude seems to have been written after many of the original apostles had died (v. 17), but no mention is made of the destruction of Jerusalem (AD 70). Many scholars think that Jude was dependent on and thus written after 2 Peter (c. AD 64–67), since verses 4–18 are somewhat parallel to 2 Peter 2:1–3:3. However, it is not clear which epistle, if either, was copied by the other (see Introduction to 2 Peter).

THEME: The importance of standing for the faith against false teachers.

PURPOSE: To encourage believers to "earnestly contend for the faith" (v. 3) by recognizing the character of false teachers and responding to their errors with perseverance in the truth and compassionate action to those endangered by heresy.

SYNOPSIS

The Contribution of Jude to Redemptive Revelation
The letter of Jude encourages believers to "contend for the faith" (v. 3) and keep themselves "in the love of God" (v. 21). Jude warns against false teachers who corrupt the gospel and deny "our Lord Jesus Christ" (v. 4), comparing them with Old Testament examples and describing them with sharp admonitions and vivid word pictures (vv. 5–16). Jude

urges believers to keep themselves from falling away and to "have compassion" on others who are in danger (vv. 22–23). The letter begins and ends with comforting truths concerning God's preservation of believers, closing with a beautiful doxology to "our Saviour" who "is able to keep you from falling" (vv. 24–25).

Theologically, Jude primarily focuses on describing false teachers and the Christian response to them (cf. 2 Thess. 2:10; 2 Peter 2:1–22; 1 John 2:18–23). The book teaches the twin doctrines of God's preservation (Jude 1–2, 24–25) and the believer's need to persevere (vv. 17–23). It also teaches the doctrine of God—especially His sovereign authority in the face of rebellion, His pending judgment of ungodliness, and His triune character (vv. 20–21). Jude also forms a basis for Christian apologetics.

Key themes of the book include:

1. Faithful Christians must remember the apostolic word (vv. 17–19), keep themselves in sound doctrine (vv. 20–21), and have compassion on the lost (vv. 22–23) in order to persevere in the faith.

2. False teachers can be identified by their denial of Christ's Lordship (unbelief, v. 4) and their immoral character (ungodliness, vv. 4–16).

3. Confessing the sovereign authority of God (vv. 5–16) and striving for personal growth in the Christian graces (vv. 3, 20–23) are antidotes against false teaching.

4. The Lord will judge false teachers and punish all rebellion at the coming judgment day (vv. 5–16).

5. Christ will keep His people from apostasy and present them without sin to God (vv. 24–25).

OUTLINE
I. Greeting (vv. 1–2)
II. Purpose (vv. 3–4)
III. Warning (vv. 5–16)
IV. Instructions (vv. 17–23)
V. Doxology (vv. 24–25)

Notes

1

2

3

4

5

Notes

6

7

8

9

10

Notes

11

12

13

14

Notes

15

16

17

18

19

20

Notes

21

22

23

24

25

STUDY QUESTIONS

1. Verse 1: What does Jude say about believers?

2. Verses 3–4: What exhortation is given here? How do we do that? Why is it necessary?

3. Verse 7: What does Jude teach about Sodom and Gomorrah?

4 Verse 11: What were the sins of these people (Gen. 4:1–8; Num. 16:1–35; 22:1–35; 31:16)?

5. Verses 14–15: Who was Enoch (Gen. 5:21–24)? What did he prophesy?

6. Verse 19: What do these false and wicked teachers lack?

7. Verses 20–21: What should believers do in response to this false teaching?

8. Verses 22–23: How should believers help others?

9. Verses 24–25: What is God able to do? Who is this God? What does He deserve?

DEVOTIONAL REFLECTIONS

1. Contending for the faith does not begin with a direct attack against error but rather with a lifestyle of godliness built on biblical truth. Personal piety is the best protection against ungodliness. The holiness of the whole church is more important than public action against error. Showing compassion to the perishing should come after we are grounded in the most holy faith and when we are actively avoiding all associations with error that tarnish our witness. How can you grow in both godliness and compassion without compromise?

2. Realize that false teachers are still in the church among the saints today. Note that Jude describes people who are presently in the church, not people who have already left the church. There will always be hypocrisy, ungodliness, and even apostate people among the gathering of believers. The church, especially its elders, should be prepared to confront error in its midst and to expel those who refuse to repent. How can you best guard yourself against false teachers?

3. Receive spiritual encouragement from God's preservation of both His church corporately and His people individually. As God delivered His people in the past, so He continues to keep His church in the present and future. Likewise, God preserves each believer individually. Though there are many causes for stumbling, believers are graciously kept from apostasy since Christ is both able and willing to keep them. God preserves His people so that they will both keep and contend for the faith. Do you feel your need for His preserving power today? Turn verses 24–25 into a prayer for yourself and your loved ones for faith and perseverance to the glory of God.